Measuring with Sebastian Pig and Friends
On a Road Trip

By Jill Anderson

Illustrated by Amy Huntington

Series Math Consultant:
Cassi Heppelmann
Elementary School Teacher
Farmington School District
Minnesota

Series Literacy Consultant:
Allan A. De Fina, Ph.D.
Dean, College of Education / Professor of Literacy Education
New Jersey City University
Past President of the New Jersey Reading Association

Enslow Elementary
an imprint of
Enslow Publishers, Inc.
40 Industrial Road
Box 398
Berkeley Heights, NJ 07922
USA

http://www.enslow.com

To Parents and Teachers:

As you read Sebastian's story with a child,

*Rely on the pictures to see the math visually represented.

*Use Sebastian's notebook, which summarizes the math at hand.

*Practice math facts with your child using the examples on page 30.

Enslow Elementary, an imprint of Enslow Publishers, Inc.

Enslow Elementary® is a registered trademark of Enslow Publishers, Inc.

Library of Congress Cataloging-in-Publication Data
Anderson, Jill, 1968-
   Measuring with Sebastian pig and friends : on a road trip / written by Jill Anderson ; illustrated by Amy Huntington.
      p. cm. – (Math fun with Sebastian pig and friends!)
   Includes index.
   Summary: "A fun and simple review of different ways to measure for beginning readers"–Provided by publisher.
   ISBN-13: 978-0-7660-3362-7
   ISBN-10: 0-7660-3362-7
   1. Measurement–Juvenile literature. I. Title.
QA465.A63 2009
516'.15–dc22
                    2008028472

Editorial Direction: Red Line Editorial, Inc.

Printed in the United States of America

10 9 8 7 6 5 4 3 2 1

To Our Readers: We have done our best to make sure all Internet Addresses in this book were active and appropriate when we went to press. However, the author and the publisher have no control and assume no liability for the material available on those Internet sites or on other Web sites they may link to. Any comments or suggestions can be sent by e-mail to comments@enslow.com or to the address on the back cover.

♻ Enslow Publishers, Inc. is committed to printing our books on recycled paper. The paper in every book contains 10% to 30% post-consumer waste (PCW). The cover board on the outside of every book contains 100% PCW. Our goal is to do our part to help young people and the environment too!

Table of Contents

It's a big day for Sebastian Pig! He and his friends are going on a road trip. They will have contests, too. Who can find the biggest things? Or the heaviest? Or the longest?

Sebastian will measure many things. Can you help him? Need a hint? Look for answers in Sebastian's notebook.

A Friendly Contest

"Wow!" Ben Bear says. "Your suitcase is big, Sebastian!"

Sebastian says, "Let's have a contest. Let's see who has the biggest suitcase!"

8

Sebastian stands next to his suitcase. It goes up to his chest. Gina Giraffe's suitcase only goes to her knee. Who will win?

Gina is taller. Her knees are high off the ground.

"We need a better way to measure!" says Sebastian.

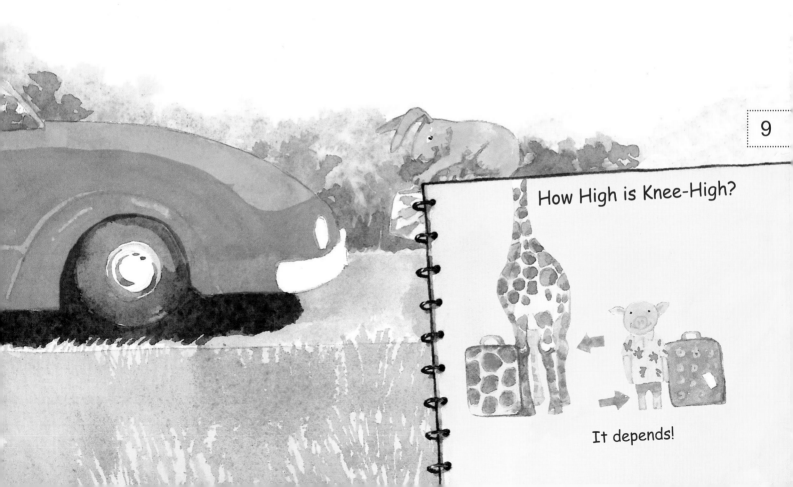

How High is Knee-High?

It depends!

Which Is Taller?

Sebastian finds a yardstick. Its numbers go from 1 to 36.

He takes the end with the 1. He puts it at the bottom of his suitcase. He holds it straight. The yardstick meets the top of the suitcase. What number is there?

"My suitcase is 30 inches tall," Sebastian says.

Gina measures her suitcase the same way. Her suitcase is 35 inches tall. "I win!" she says.

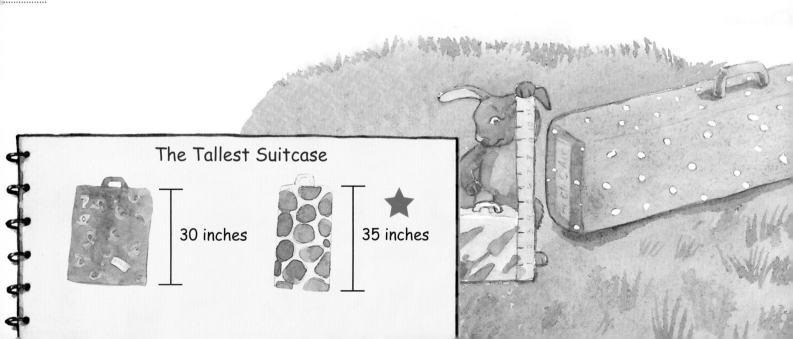

The Tallest Suitcase

30 inches

35 inches

Ben turns the yardstick over. This side has numbers, too.

"Those are for centimeters," Sebastian says. "A centimeter is smaller than an inch."

Sebastian measures the suitcases again. This time he uses centimeters. Gina is still the winner.

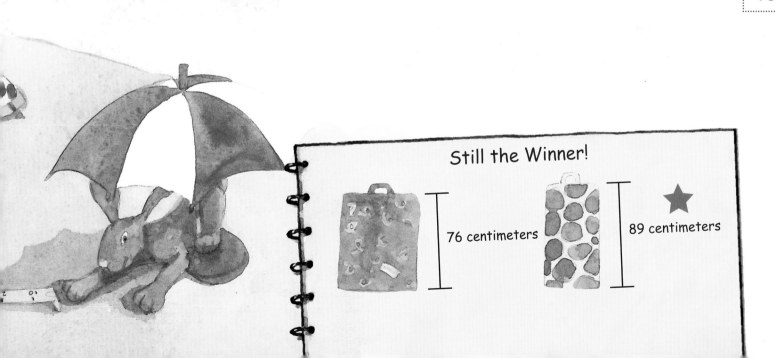

Still the Winner!

76 centimeters

89 centimeters

On the Scale

Gina's suitcase is the tallest. But whose is the heaviest?

Sebastian gets his bathroom scale. He sets each suitcase on the scale. The arrow points to the number 40. "Forty pounds!" Sebastian says. He is the winner!

The Heaviest Suitcase

★ 40 pounds

23 pounds

ROCKS
50 pounds

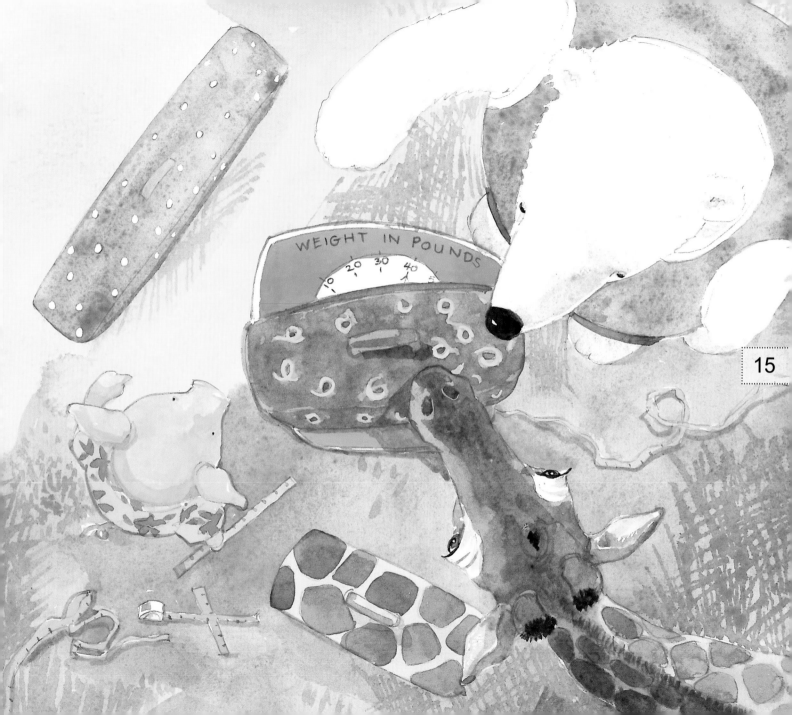

A Pound of Candy

It's time to hit the road! The first stop is the Chocolate House. Yum!

Gina sees a giant chocolate bar. It is one pound.

Wait a minute. Gina looks at the candy bar again. Why does it say 16?

"That's for 16 ounces," Sebastian says. "Sixteen ounces equal one whole pound!"

The Heaviest Chocolate Bar

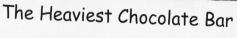 = 16 ounces

MILK CHOCOLATE RHINO 6 OUNCES

Twists and Turns

The next stop is the water park. The friends go on three water slides. Ready, set, go! They're off!

Sebastian hits the water first, then Gina. Ben hits last. Why didn't they all hit the water together?

Gina knows. "Ben's slide has the most turns. That makes it the longest!"

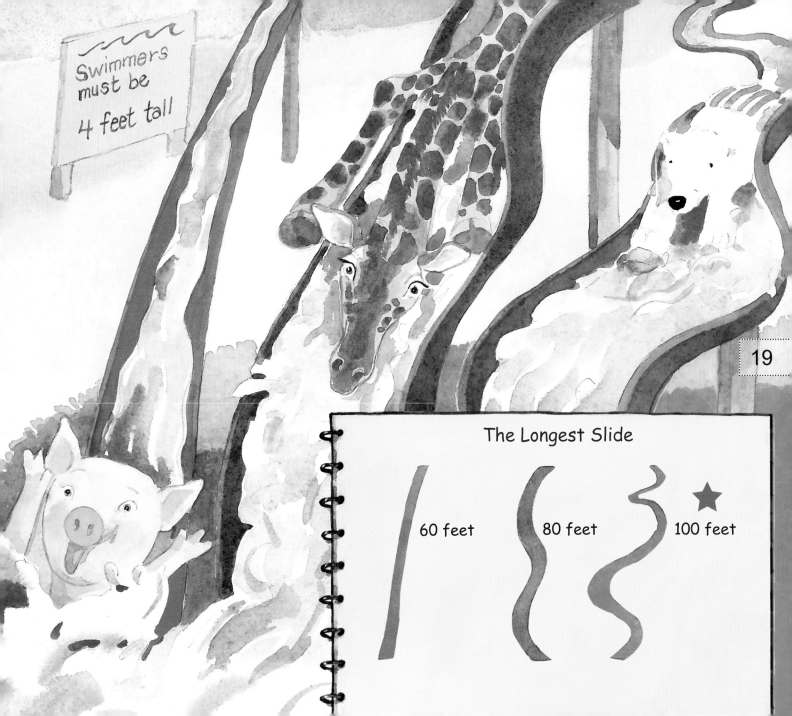

Swimmers must be 4 feet tall

The Longest Slide

60 feet 80 feet 100 feet ★

20

Flying Footballs

Now they are at a sports show. There is a contest. Who can throw the farthest? Ben steps up to the line. He throws the football. It goes WAY down the field!

Ben's pass is 60 yards long. He wins!

The Longest Pass

60 ← 60 yards

50

40

30

20

10

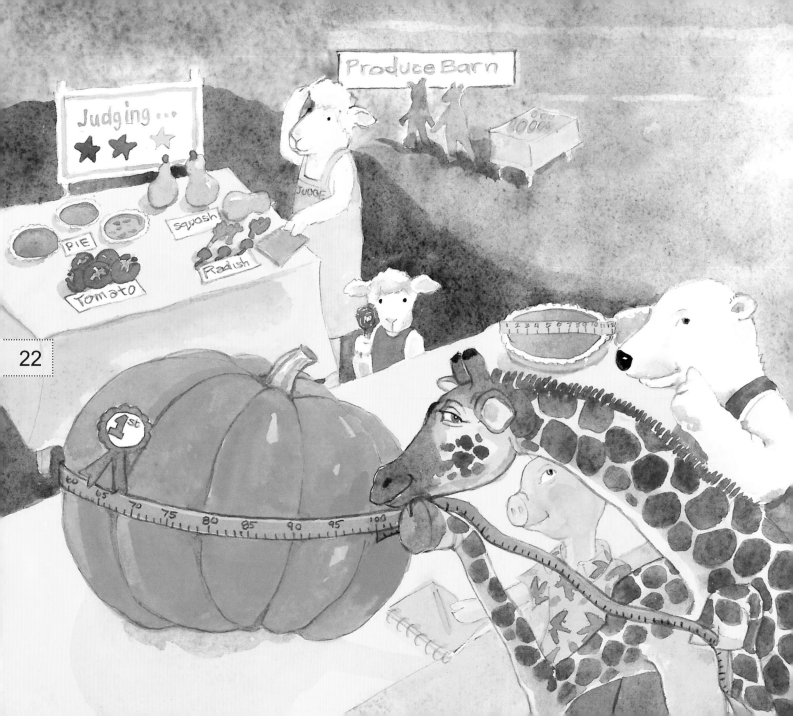

22

The Biggest Pumpkin

The friends go to a fair. Pumpkins are everywhere.
There will be a prize for the biggest one. Which one is it?
Gina will find out.

"How do you measure round things?" she asks.

Ben sees a pumpkin pie. It is round. He holds a ruler across
its top. "This way!" he says.

"No, no," Gina says. She does not want to measure the top of
the pumpkin. She wants to measure around it.

"I know!" she says. She takes the tape measure. She wraps it
around each pumpkin, like a belt. She finds the biggest one!

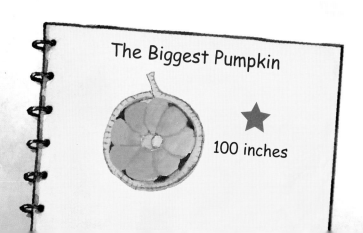

The Biggest Pumpkin

★ 100 inches

A Good Guess

The next stop is Dinosaur-o-rama. There are dinosaurs everywhere.

Sebastian looks at the meat eaters. He likes the Allosaurus. How long is it? He cannot see the sign.

He makes a guess. There is a leg bone. It is one yard long. Sebastian thinks about putting the leg bones in a line. The line goes along the dinosaur's body. How many bones are there? Sebastian guesses Allosaurus is about 10 bones long.

It is a good guess! The sign says that this Allosaurus is 11 yards long.

The Longest Meat Eater

11 yards

1 yard

Bunnysaurus
1 Foot

Two Ways to Try

The friends are ready for a walk. Which way is the lake?
Gina looks at the map.

There are two walks. The north path is 100 yards long.
The south path is 200 feet. Which one is longer?

"Well, 200 is more than 100," Ben says.

But the biggest number is not always the winner. A yard is
longer than a foot. At 100 yards, the north path is the winner!

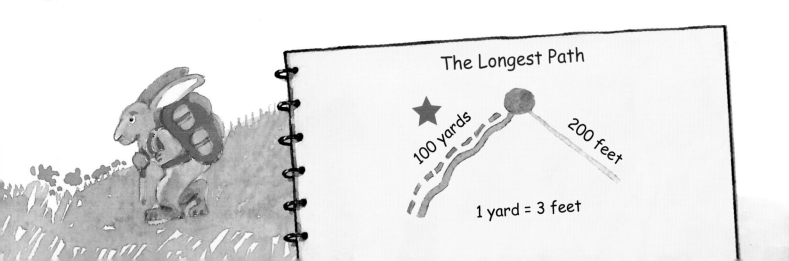

The Longest Path

100 yards

200 feet

1 yard = 3 feet

The sun is setting. Sebastian and his friends are going home. He thinks of all they have seen—and measured!

Now You Know

A centimeter is less than an inch.

One foot is 12 inches.

One yard is three feet.

One pound is 16 ounces.

Words to Know

centimeter—a unit to measure length that is a little less than half an inch long; a centimeter is from a system of measuring called the metric system.

foot—a unit of measure. Twelve inches equal one foot.

inch—a unit of measure. One inch is 1/12 of a foot.

ounce—a unit to measure weight, often used for food; 16 ounces equal one pound.

yard—a unit of measure. Thirty-six inches equal a yard.

Learn More

Books

Hirschmann, Kris. *The Dog: Is a Paw a Foot?* New York: Scholastic, 2005.

Murphy, Patricia J. *Measuring Puppies and Kittens*. Berkeley Heights, NJ: Enslow, 2008.

Web Sites

Cool Math
http://www.Coolmath4kids.com

KidPort
http://www.kidport.com

Index